KING

Four-Part Leadership Framework for Black Men

*"All kings are not born of royal bloodlines. Some become royal because of what they do **once they realize who they are**."*
~ Pharrell Williams

Dr. Ian P. Buchanan

King, Four-Part Leadership Framework for Black Men

Copyright © 2022 Ian P. Buchanan, EdD

All rights reserved. No part of this book may be reproduced in any form or by any electronic or mechanical means including information storage and retrieval systems without permission in writing from the publisher, except by a reviewer, who may quote brief passages in a review.

Published in the United States, Nia Education Group

DocBuchanan.com

First Edition

Library of Congress 2022912577

ISBN 978-1-957904-05-4

"We are living in impossible times. If it were fiction, it would be critiqued as hyperbolic. If it were nightmares, we would never sleep. We are living in times created by our own species…our visions are ropes through the devastation. Look further ahead, like our ancestors did, look further. Extend, hold on, pull, evolve."
– Adrienne Maree Brown

Dedication

I am grateful to have the ancestors upon whose shoulders I stand. This book is dedicated to the legacies of those ancestors - my grandmothers, grandfathers, uncles, and aunties. Grandmother, Big Mama, Mama Sam, Grandaddy, Papa, Aunt Dee Dee, Aunt Prit, Aunt Andrea, Uncle Vernon...all y'all.

King is also dedicated to the brothers who are committed to shaking up the world. *King* is written *for us, by us*, and *with us in mind*. Our voices matter. Our perspectives matter. Our leadership matters. Within the dedication to my brothers, there is also a challenge. I challenge you to use this book to do two things: reflect and act. When you reflect, I challenge you to truthfully interrogate yourself while also giving yourself grace. When you act, I challenge you to influence and inspire change in a way that slashes the tires of white supremacy. Action for action's sake is not enough. We must change the game and interrupt the structures and systems that keep a knee on our collective necks. Our leadership is crucial.

Last, *King* is dedicated to the family who has had my back for so long. My queen, Carmen, is ride or die, and I wouldn't be able to move without her love and support. She is an angel on earth. Nia, my baby girl, is a loving human being who embodies excellence and understands her purpose. My siblings inspire and teach me.

...and of course, Dear Mama, I gotta thank the Lord that you made me!

Table of Contents

Introduction

What is a Kingmaker?

"My only goal (is) to make a real n***a feel seen." – Jay Z

Many of my brothers never get clear about their real leadership superpowers. We never quite figure out the unique contribution our leadership *makes* on the world…or *can potentially make* on the world. Sometimes, it seems that only athletes and artists are clear about their superpowers. Jordan knows he is the GOAT (don't debate me). Jay is well aware that he is J-Hova. Miles knew he was the coolest of the cool. The late Jean-Michel Basquiat, whose paintings sold for more than 100 million dollars, had to know he was in a totally different artistic stratosphere.

As a professional and education leader for more than two decades, I've known for a while that I had strengths, but I never could quite put my hands on my real leadership superpowers. I was too busy stressing about my leadership shortcomings, trying to execute a leadership playbook that was not designed for my leadership game, and treading the tumultuous terrain of leadership. Admittedly, I was even my own kryptonite sometimes.

It took several decades of trials and tribulations to understand my leadership superpowers and my leadership kryptonite. A few very few specific events, however, transformed me as a leader and as a human being. I realized that I was overly consumed by my leadership shortcomings. I realized that I was trying to execute a leadership "playbook" that did not serve me or my people. I realized that I was not always doing the work that was best for my mental and/or physical wellness. Lastly, I realized I was increasingly becoming more disconnected from my strengths, my values, and my purpose.

Now, I see! For so long, I had been trying to understand my place in the world's infinite space, negotiating the tension between being confident in my purpose without being perceived as arrogant, vain, or self-consumed. Now, IDGAF what "they" think. I am now clear that my purpose, mission, and leadership superpower can be summarized by one word: **Kingmaker.**

The Black Kingmaker

♦ ♦ ♦

Suppose you heard someone refer to themselves as Kingmaker, especially absent of context. In that case, there could likely be several thoughts running through your head. You might say, "That sounds like an arrogant self-description." You might also say, "That sounds cool, but I am not clear about what the term Kingmaker *really* means." Admittedly, when I first heard the term in context, I was intrigued to know what it meant. More specifically, I began to think about how the concept of Kingmaker might apply to modern leadership.

I first heard the term Kingmaker in 2015, when I came across an astute young brother, Ken Thomas. A 30-something, super confident Southerner, Ken seemed to be wise beyond his years. Like Dr. Martin Luther King, Jr., Ken was a man of Alpha Phi Alpha and an ordained minister, but he added his special skinny-leg pants wearing, millennial spin to the game. Upon introducing himself to our cohort of Leadership Memphis Fellowship participants, Ken delivered his pitch: "I'm Ken, and I'm the CEO of Kingmakers...I make kings. I put people in position to gain political influence and power. I help people leverage their values and strengths to make an impact through politics. My ultimate goal is to do in politics what Bayard Rustin did for the Civil Rights Movement."

When Ken died suddenly in 2020, I was crushed, and so were so many others. The social media world's outpouring of love and respect for Ken came from all walks of life - but it especially came from his people. It was a true testimonial to who Ken really was, a Kingmaker.

I began to reflect more deeply and intentionally on the term Kingmaker, specifically thinking about how it applies to my journey as a leader and servant. Suddenly, I was able to view my leadership, vision, and purpose from a different and deeper vantage point.

As I reflected on my leadership journey, two things became crystal clear to me. First, I became clear about who I *am* and who I *am not* – as a leader and as a person. My purpose is not to be the world's latest version of Jay - Z, Miles, or Basquiat. In retrospect, my leadership journey helped me realize that the late Tupac Shakur and I share a similar personal vision: "I'm not saying I'm gonna change the world, but I guarantee that I will spark the brain that will change the world."

Like my brother Ken, I am committed to Kingmaking. That is, I am committed to providing support and guidance that helps great leaders be the greatest they can be. I want Kings to be Kings. Yep, I'm talking to you, King.

"Humbly, Nah respectfully." – Jay Z

A Book for the Kings

"The homie said, Hov, it ain't many of us. I told him less is more, my n$$$a, it's plenty of us." – Jay Z

When I began this writing journey with my first writing coach, the first thing she asked was, **Why** are you writing this book? This is undoubtedly a valid and important question. Another equally important question is just as simple. That simple question is, "**Who** is the target audience?"

Said in another way, "*Bro, who you writin' this book for?*"

The **why** is important, but the **who** is more important, in the case of *King*. The target audience is more important in the case of *King* because the multiple perspectives of this particular group are rarely elevated in leadership spaces. When I considered writing this book, the target audience, the **who**, came to me in an undeniable way.

When I decided to author this book, I focused on a specific group...brothers. Brothers, this book is **for** you and **to** you. While this book can engage, inspire, inform, and challenge a whole lot of folks, **I wrote *King* specifically to black and brown leaders working in education.** These leaders might work in any number of areas, including traditional public schools, charters, independents, parochial, nonprofit organizations, higher education, adult education, education policy, education technology, education entrepreneurship - any aspect of the education ecosystem. Although this book was written with a specific group in mind, **it has jewels for all black men doing the leadership thing**.

To be specific, when I wrote *King*, I imagined that I was writing this book to an inspiring group of young black male leaders I had recently encountered at an event in the St. Louis area.

The Kings Who Inspired Me to Write This Book

In July of 2018, I was invited to attend a social networking event comprised mostly of black male educators who had recently joined the education leadership ranks – or who were aspiring to do so. Of the approximately 40 attendees, the great majority of them were in their 30s.

Drs. Howard Fields and Daryl Diggs, the conveners of this social networking event, were rolling out the Black Male Educators - St. Louis (BME-STL) organization, a nationally affiliated collaborative committed to uplifting black male educators and disrupting inequity in education. I was excited to join this group of brothers committed to impacting lives. Immediately, I was committed to supporting the leadership and the mission of BME-STL.

As I entered the rather large venue and began working my way towards the reserved BME-STL section, one thing became clear almost immediately. In a room filled with black male leaders in education, I was one of **the** oldest brothers in the room. Times had indeed changed before my eyes and in many ways. Looking at these guys was like looking in the mirror...**at the old me**. The aggressive, vocal, borderline-arrogant "young gun" that used to be Ian Buchanan has gone to pasture. As a young leader, I learned a lot and worked with great teams...to make some real impact on the game. At the same time, I've endured my fair share of leadership bumps and bruises along the way. *For real.*

The **old us** must get out of the way so the new us can present itself. The old Ian has been replaced with a more deliberate, reflective, knowledgeable practitioner who is less attention-seeking. Through a lot of self-work, the ego has taken a back seat, and I have become laser-focused on being the "drum major for justice" that Dr. King urged us to be. In version 2.0 of my leadership dictionary, **we** now takes precedence over **me**. That was not always true. *I'm just keepin' it a buck...*

In so many ways, I see the promise and energy of the old Ian Buchanan in this group (minus the bad shhh). These black men will have journeys and experiences eerily similar to mine - but not identical to mine. These younger brothers are moving to the peaks of their leadership careers, and their energy is affirming, supporting, and pretty damn magical. At the same time, I know that each of them will encounter challenges that will make their knees buckle. *For real.*

While being one of the oldest in the space was very different and slightly uncomfortable for me, it was an awesome opportunity for me to listen and learn. As the event moved on and conversations ensued, I listened to many brothers share their stories, aspirations, challenges, and even vulnerabilities. I began to experience a mix of emotions. I reflected on my past experiences and was able to connect in a way that deeply touched my soul…and lit a fire under me.

I wanted to support and engage with every brother in the room. The problem-solver in me wanted to offer thoughts, suggestions, and reflection questions to help each brother in the room reach his full potential. I wanted to help these men continue to be great.

King is written to inspire the brothers in that room and the thousands of black male leaders across the country who are making "good trouble." *King* is for the brothers who are swimming in the deep waters of a racist ocean.

As I reflect on the stories and professional journeys of the kings I engaged with during the BME-STL event, I break those convos down into three distinct categories: brothers who **got next**, brothers who **got now**, and brothers who **feel like the Other.** *King* is written **to** and **for** each of these groups of brothers.

Kings Who "Got Next"

Growing up in the late 80s, two things were pretty popular among my adolescent peers: sports and video games. In fact, outside of conversations about young ladies, sports and video games consumed most of our daily conversations and activities. After school, we would regularly engage in sports activities like 21, Horse, and "Court" Ball. In addition to playing sports, we would spend hours playing video games like Pac-Man, Donkey Kong, Galaga, Centipede, and handheld Coleco Football.

As I recall, there was often a queue, or waitlist, related to our sports and video game contests. Similar to a waitlist you might find at a crowded restaurant, there was always a wait list to participate in a game of 21 or a game of Pac-Man. Since there was usually a wait, you would have to verbally express your desire to play by saying three words: "I got next." In essence, you were reserving your space in the queue. You were proclaiming your interest in entering "the arena."

Signifying that you got next does not only mean that you want to enter the arena, but it also signifies a belief in your ability to hold your own. Calling next means you have developed a level of self-confidence, and you're betting on yourself. Calling next means that you are committed to developing the skill it requires to keep winning, even when the competition gets better.

King is for those leaders who are calling next. If you are in the midst of a professional transition, that means you are calling next. You may be on track to take a position as chair of the English department, or you may be an assistant principal on your way to becoming a head principal. You may be in a D9 fraternity, strolling at your last few college kickbacks, and you are trying to make your first big career move. **King, this is for you**.

Kings Who "Got Now"

As a brother who has served for three decades, I have been enriched by brothers who have had both similar and very different leadership journeys than I've had. Those life and leadership experiences that make us unique are the same ones that can also be inspiring and affirming to other brothers - no matter where they are along their respective leadership journeys. Our differences, if leveraged effectively, can make us more impactful leaders than we could ever imagine.

Surely, as leaders, brothers have unique journeys. Indeed, no group is a monolith. Far too often, across the board, brothers who serve in **any** leadership capacity will experience **many** common challenges. White supremacy is omnipresent in every leadership room, no matter who sits at the leadership table. Racism, power, privilege, and stereotype come together like a wicked four-headed monster to unleash on black men. The weight can get heavy for each and every one of us.

Like many brothers currently assuming leadership roles, I understand the weightiness of the work…and I carry it. Far too often, I don't carry it as well as I would like.

This book is written for the brothers who are metaphorically alongside me and alongside us, carrying that weight and embracing what it means to be a servant and leader. You are the brothers who got now.

The brothers who got now must continue to support and enrich the brothers who got next…and vice versa. We have a mutually shared responsibility. As summarized succinctly and powerfully in Proverbs 27:17, *"Iron sharpeneth iron, so a man sharpeneth the countenance of his friend."* We have a wealth of experience, wisdom, and technical skills. We can continue to make each other better.

13

King is written to help brothers who got now become even more powerful and transformational.

This book is helpful for brothers who got now (the brothers currently in the field) because it affirms parts of your leadership stories and experiences. *King* will also challenge you. Black and brown male leaders' stories, experiences, and perspectives are not usually told in first-person, authentic ways. This book affirms the brothers who are currently holding down the leadership crown. **You matter, and this book is written because you matter.**

Kings Who Feel Like the "Other"

King is not written to suggest a normative definition of black maleness or black male leadership. I contend that narrow definitions of black maleness are not helpful to our cause overall…especially if we cannot demonstrate our full humanity to all. We must make a loving, non-judgmental, and supportive space for *us all*.

Sometimes, without malicious intent, groups of brothers can push other brothers' contributions and voices to the margins. We are guilty of this when we narrowly and normatively define black manhood. We become "realness regulators." By confining *any* human to a narrow, subjective definition of what it means to be human, we rob them of pieces of their humanity…and our own. *Get out people's shit.*

When we create restrictive definitions of what it means to be a "real" black man, we dehumanize ourselves and minimize our potential for collective impact. Again, we must make a loving, non-judgmental, and supportive space for *us all*. Othering each other is another way we make internalized oppression real. *Ain't nobody got time for that.*

Undoubtedly, the most persistent, resistant, and significant Othering comes from the American caste system that advantages and disadvantages folks based on race. Our white colleagues are benefactors of a purposefully-designed, inequitable system. There are too many cases in leadership spaces where mental models, policies, and practices are angled against black and brown leaders...and towards white folks.

While some white leaders have good intentions, intentions and outcomes are two very different things. Far too many black and brown leaders enter predominantly white environments feeling a sense of discomfort, insecurity, or a need to be the perfect representation of their "people." Sometimes, we strive hard to **be like** in order to **be.**

Unfortunately, the professional trauma we experience by being Othered *inside* of the workplace is eerily similar to some of the traumas we feel *outside* of the workplace. This reality is far too common...and has existed far too long. The feeling that Othering gives us was captured perfectly in 1957 by James Baldwin when he said, "To be a Negro in this country and to be relatively conscious is to be in a state of rage almost, almost all of the time."

This book is written **for** and **to** brothers in leadership who have felt like the Other. *King* is written to affirm your experiences. If you are not sure if you fit into the Other category, I have provided some clues for you.

- You had to conform to fit into someone else's definition of leadership at some point. In order to **be**, you had to **be like**. In doing so, you felt like a fish out of water…and maybe even a sellout.
- You felt like you had to turn down your authentic blackness to be heard and validated.
- You challenged a racist or otherwise xenophobic statement…and then you became the bad guy.
- You were asked to (or felt compelled to) speak as a representative for all people who share one of your identities. For instance, you had become the "race representative."
- You were conscious about talking, looking, or dressing "too black" or "not black enough."
- Something was said or done that reminded you that you were the "only one" in the room.
- You experienced a micro-aggression…again.

In conclusion, *King,* is written **to** and **for** a broad range of leaders. It is written for both veterans and early professionals. It is written for those who are current leaders, those who are transitioning into new leadership roles, and those who sometimes feel professionally isolated. If you got now, got next, or feel like an Other, this book is for you. This book is for *errrrbody*…all of us who are in (or desire to be in) the arena of leadership.

King's Undergirding Beliefs and Understandings

♦♦♦

Wicked Problem

The KING Leadership Framework is undergirded by three guiding beliefs and understandings:

1. The wicked problems leaders face today are unprecedented.
2. Race matters, and we take an abolitionist perspective on race.
3. We remain eternally hopeful and strategic.

In the mid-1970s, architecture design theorist Jakob Rittel defined the term *wicked problem* as a social or cultural problem that is almost impossible to solve. Rittel suggests that a wicked problem has four primary characteristics.

1. **Enormity of the problem.** The problem is multi-layered...and huge.
2. **Lack of consensus around solutions.** There are multiple, sometimes-contradictory perspectives around solutions to the problem.
3. **Expense.** Addressing the root causes of the problem is exorbitantly expensive.

4. **No blueprint**. There is no precedent or blueprint available to inform a solution. No one has solved "this" before.

As leaders, we are in the throes of a uniquely wicked problem. There has never been such a time as this for anyone, but especially for those in the crosshairs of leadership. Covid scares, racism, politics, and killings have been a part of our daily lives...concurrently. For many of us, we have also experienced unimaginable personal and professional trauma over the last few years.

As a certified leadership coach and education vet who works alongside a broad cross-section of leaders, I hear a lot. I hear the stories of exhaustion, stress, family sacrifice, health scares, and struggle. Especially in the Covid era, leadership is tough. In the worlds of many of my people in leadership, there are certain songs that stay on our playlist...especially on the way to work. Kenrick Lamar's "We Gon' Be Aight" and Tupac's "Me Against the World" are the songs that keep us from snappin' on somebody.

The KING Leadership Framework was developed with a clear understanding that leaders in this era face uniquely wicked challenges. Navigating leadership terrain amidst the impact of Trump, Covid variants, the Big Resignation, *and* the injustice system is the very definition of leading in unchartered waters.

No matter how robust, comprehensive, or well-meaning one may be, there is no strategic plan, framework, or algorithm that has solved our leadership Rubik's Cubes. Said differently, *this ish is different*.

Given our realities, The KING Leadership Framework will not solve the numerous wicked problems you face. Nor does it purport to provide a magic wand to impact the fog of racism – which is at the root of the majority of our challenges. *King* does provide a framework to help you: a) explore and reflect on your full brilliance as a leader, b) strengthen your leadership resilience, and c) supplement your toolkit of transferrable leadership skills.

Upon adapting the framework to your unique personal and professional profile, you will lead more authentically and impactfully as you confront your wicked leadership challenges.

Four-Part Leadership Framework for Black Men

Race Matters

In his song, "War," Bob Marley borrows from Emperor Haile Selassie of Ethiopia when he envisions a world where"…the color of a man's skin is no more significant than the color of his eyes." As leaders, we appreciate the liberatory vision Marley and Selassie describe. That should be every human's end goal. We must acknowledge, though, that the permanence of race and racism make our wicked problems even more wicked. **Race matters. Period.**

One of the premises of Critical Race Theory (CRT) that grounds this text is that racism is an ever-present reality in our country. In *Why Are All the Black Kids Sitting Together in the Cafeteria?*, Dr. Beverly Tatum calls racism an omniscient and omnipresent "smog" that poisons us all. It's an unfortunate, but true reality. The wicked problem of educational inequity is a direct result of the white supremacist ideologies that support, sustain, and reproduce the same results…over and over. Indeed, the school classroom is just one room in the large house that sits at 1619 Racist Avenue.

The KING Framework is written with the clear understanding that we confront a unique set of wicked problems. In addition, we understand that race and leadership cannot be decoupled. In leadership, race matters. Period.

Racism in education plays itself out for black and brown leaders in several ways. Broadly speaking, most explain racial disparities in education by adopting either of two perspectives. Both perspectives are implications of the impact of racism's smog.

Ways to Explain Racial Differences in Performance

The Pathology Perspective

The first perspective is the pathology perspective. This perspective is undergirded by a white supremacist ideology that normalizes racial inequity. In essence, the pathology perspective argues that something is wrong with **those** people. The only way for this pathology to sustain itself is that it must assign differences in achievement to racial or cultural deficits. Instead of indicting the racist system that has produced inequities, the pathology perspective lulls us into believing that racial performance gaps are "just the way it is" and "that's just the way **they** (**we**) are." **Those** people have character defects that limit them from performing equally. If **those** people would only _____ harder…

To those who agree with the pathology perspective, differences in third-grade reading proficiency, high school graduation rates, college readiness, and SAT scores have little to do with the impact of racism. Instead, these individuals would assign the differences to a commonly used set of cultural pathologies.

It must be noted that adopters of the cultural pathology perspective are not necessarily racists…**and they are not necessarily white**. We all breathe the smog of racism. For people of color, the outcome of breathing the smog of racism is internalized oppression, which can result in Othering *those* black folks, and even performing what sociologists call "horizontal violence."

No matter the racial identity, we often hear adopters of the cultural pathology perspective saying things like:

- "Those people just don't have their priorities together. They'd rather focus on ..."
- "Things have changed since they moved into the area."
- "The problem is that those parents..."
- "They don't take education seriously."
- "If the kids would just pull their pants up..."
- "This community has really declined since..."
- "If they can learn all those rap songs, they can learn how to read and write."
- "The new (black/brown) leadership doesn't know what they are doing."

If you align with this perspective, you believe that there is something inherently dysfunctional ingrained in a specific culture or race.

This perspective, the pathology perspective, represents just one explanation of racial differences in performance. There is a second perspective, and it rejects the notion that black and brown people's underperformance is a result of their own racial, cultural, or personal deficits. *We ain't broke.*

The Abolitionist Perspective

A second way to explain racial performance differentials is the abolitionist perspective. From this perspective, leadership actions are driven by a justice-centered, "we have nothing to lose but our chains" vibe. Specifically related to education, the perspective is grounded in a deep understanding of the relationship between racial **injustice** and the educational empowerment of black and brown students. The perspective acknowledges the impact of racism, but it also sees black and brown people as victors, not victims. Abolitionists see racism as an "unacceptable injustice."

In the Netflix series, *#blackAF*, scriptwriter Kenya Barris coins a simple phrase that explains almost every messed-up situation black folks find themselves in: "because of slavery." To explain the "because of slavery" sentiment in just a few words could not do it justice. Perhaps, though, the words of Malcolm X can provide some additional clarity.

In a speech he made one month before he was assassinated in 1965, Malcolm X offered "...that we were black people in a racist society. We were black people in a society whose very political system was steeped and nourished upon racism. Whose social system was a racist system. Whose economic system was nourished with racism." In other words, the foundation of *every* institution is steeped in racism, so it makes sense that an imbalanced education system would produce imbalanced results.

The proponents of the abolitionist perspective deeply understand the "because of slavery" reality. To confront the reality and to interrupt racial inequality, the abolitionist perspective prioritizes self-definition, self-determination, and thoughtful strategy. As explained by Bettina Love, in *We Want to Do More Than Survive: Abolitionist Teaching and the Pursuit of Educational Freedom*, the abolitionist perspective… "is a way of life, a way of seeing the world, and a way of taking action against injustice. It seeks to resist, agitate, and tear down the educational survival complex…while simultaneously freedom dreaming and vigorously creating a vision for what schools will be when the educational survival complex is destroyed."

The King Leadership Framework is undergirded by the premise that race matters in leadership, and specifically in education leadership. We understand that all leaders embrace beliefs and perspectives related to race, racism, and culture. Those beliefs and perspectives directly influence leadership actions (and inactions).

Education leaders do not just adopt one of these perspectives. We are confronted with *both* on almost a daily basis. We are socialized in a country where white racist ideology is not the shark…it's the water. White racist ideology is not the wind…it's the atmosphere. While we fight against the tide, racist ideology will indeed impact our attitudes, beliefs, and actions as we lead. **Despite this reality, we do not blame our people (students and families) for being chewed up and spit out by racism.**

In *King*, we explicitly reject the pathology perspective. We will not sip the "black, brown, and broken" Cool-Aid. Being receptive to the pathology perspective is to ignore the pernicious impact of the white supremacy ideology that upholds structural and systemic racism.

Instead of adopting the "black, brown, and broken" perspective, we argue that education leaders must adopt the abolitionist perspective if we are to help create a new, more just reality for those we serve. We cannot imagine freedom from any other perspective. *This is the way.*

To co-create a new reality, our leadership must sustain an educational system grounded in our truth, our definitions of equity, and our definition of cultural relevance. As Dr. Bettina Love argues, "A truthful, equitable and culturally appropriate education is understood to be a basic human right and not only a condition of Black people's individual success and collective survival. It is also fundamental to civilization and human freedom."

The KING Leadership Framework is developed with the abolitionist perspective at its core. The framework is designed to help leaders confront oppressive structures while also confronting the self-saboteur – which is typically brought on by the impact of internalized oppression on the black, brown, poor…and not so poor.

Despite the odds, we remain hopeful…and strategic.

Servant leaders of this era are confronted with an uber-wicked set of problems, most compounded by race. Wicked problems and racism are not new to our people. *We been*

27

doin' this. The abolitionist perspective is not new, either. *We been doin' that too.* Throughout our movements for equity and justice in this country, we have always confronted the challenges brought upon by personal, structural, and institutional racism. Any liberatory, freedom-oriented movement of black or brown people in our country has been bolstered by two equally important elements: *hope and creative strategy.*

The KING Framework is grounded in the belief that we must always remain hopeful while also being strategic and creative. Nonetheless, we understand that hope is not a strategy. We desire equity and justice, and it must be grounded in thoughtful action to *get us free.*

As leaders have done throughout the Diaspora, we appreciate the importance of faith and hope. Employing faith and hope has sustained leaders of color in some of the most unbearable systems and situations.

We have consistently demonstrated a commitment to strategy as well. We do faith *and* work, hope *and* strategy. Ask the Underground Freedom Movement about Tubman. Ask the Civil Rights Movement about Bayard Rustin. Ask apartheid about the ANC and Mandela. We know hope. We also know strategy.

The KING Leadership Framework is predicated on the belief that our leadership must be driven by strategy, skill, and knowledge. We must strive towards executing with excellence. At the same time, we must lead with a belief that change is possible, despite wicked problems.

The KING approach consists of four broad, crucial leadership actions. In subsequent chapters, we provide a set of "King Moves" – strategies that will help you personalize, then operationalize.

1. **Know** the King Within
2. **Inspire** Greatness in Others for Greater Collective Impact
3. **Navigate** North
4. **Gravitate** to Great

Know the King Within

Leaders must do the deep personal work…first. Continuous personal and professional introspection are keys to serving and leading others. Constant personal introspection can inspire transformational growth - even if the growth is catalyzed by discomfort. Understanding your leadership superpowers, technical strengths, opportunities for growth, biases, emotional triggers, and self-sabotaging behaviors can help you get clear about who your authentic, supreme self really is. Once we see better, we can do better.

Inspire Greatness in Others for Greater Collective Impact

Leaders find ways to help others self-actualize, and they view intentional capacity-building as a cornerstone of leadership. Understanding that individual capacity-building can accelerate and multiply overall organizational growth, leaders move the work forward by using a distributive leadership approach. A leader is the invaluable point guard on an NBA championship team.

Navigate North

Leaders have a clear set of values and principles that guide how they choose to invest their attention, energy and focus. Leaders have a North Star (or **why**) that inspires, affirms, and influences them. For leaders in justice work, navigating north means that principles of justice determine *what they do* and *how they do it*. The mindsets and actions that do not correlate with the leader's North Star can cause unnecessary dissonance, regret, and horrible results.

Gravitate to Great

Leaders spend purposeful time in community with those who inspire, affirm, support, challenge, and model. Leaders nurture authentic, symbiotic relationships with those who embody extraordinary vision, undeniable purpose, or an unyielding commitment to excellence.

The KING Framework is grounded in experience, deep academic scholarship, and an unwavering commitment to black and brown leaders. This book is designed to help us continue to be impactful, fulfilled, and whole – understanding that black and brown leaders confront a unique set of wicked problems.

The KING Framework is adaptive. That is, you will personalize and adapt the KING approach to leverage and stretch the greatness that already exists *within you*. The KING Framework is not a formulaic, prescriptive checklist of actions that will transform you into the Steph Curry of leadership…at least not overnight.

When you walk away from the book, you should be able to:

1. **View the "king in the mirror" more clearly, more deeply, and more honestly than you ever have.**

When we are in our respective leadership "zones," our greatest strengths are sometimes "just what we do." Quite often, we don't see our leadership superpowers until others point them out. Some of us may be aware of our strengths and superpowers, but yet we may still be unsure about how to leverage them fully. It's the "knowing-doing" gap thing.

The KING Framework provides an opportunity for you to get clearer on the leadership superpowers that make you a unique gift. The framework helps you see your custom-fit leadership crown. You will be clear about how your leadership superpowers can continue to help you thrive – both professionally and personally. Then, you can leverage your knowledge to multiply your impact – while prioritizing wellness and joy.

2. **Confront self-limiting mindsets, assumptions, and behaviors.**

Most leaders have experienced self-doubt and insecurities. At some point, many of us ask questions like, "Am I really good enough to be **here**?"

The **"Am I good enough?"** sentiment goes by a variety of names, including Imposter Syndrome. When we encounter feelings like stress, anxiety, and the fear of being

31

"exposed," our brain overcompensates and injects self-limiting beliefs into our psyche. As a result of self-limiting thinking, we become our own self-sabotaging worst enemy.

As leaders, we must confront self-sabotaging thinking because it leads to self-sabotaging actions. Black leaders must know that many of the insecurities we experience are "because of slavery." That is, because of racialized conditioning, we are hypnotized by white supremacist ideologies to believe we are less.

We must interrogate the role of internalized oppression in our leadership stances. The KING Framework helps you explore some of the troubling mindsets and behaviors that influence your ability to reach your fullest leadership potential. As you courageously confront your self-limiting mindsets, assumptions, and behaviors, you will come out "on the other side" a more powerful leader. As the great Susan Taylor says, "Whatever we believe about ourselves and our ability comes true for us."

3. **Nurture the powerful relationships and networks that help you realize your "why."**

Genuine concern and love for people is what drives servant leadership. Servant leaders prioritize mission-aligned relationships, partnerships, and coalitions. Kings are strategic about developing and nurturing professional affiliations that help them impact the greater good.

Relationships are never one-way. As leaders, we must commit to sharpening others, and we must also commit to being sharpened. As leaders, we see potential value in *every* relationship and interaction. We also understand that our purpose is to make measurable impact. Our **why** influences our leadership walk and how we engage the people along our respective journeys.

The KING approach helps you best leverage relationships, partnerships, and coalitions - for the greater good. You will leverage a 360-degree view of yourself to get clearer about the individuals, environments, energies, and competencies that will help you reach your leadership high score.

4. **Strategically leverage your "why" to become your best leadership self.**

When we lead and make decisions that align with our values, gifts, and talents, our life has a positive and invigorating energy. On the other hand, when **what** we do is grossly inconsistent with our **why**, life starts to get ugly. At this point, leadership can feel a lot like professional purgatory.

The KING Framework helps you consider ways to best match your **what** to your **why**. You will use strategic thinking protocols to ensure that your **why** and **what** are connected. Your leadership actions will be more equivalent to **who you are** and **why you are committed**.

Four-Part Leadership Framework for Black Men

The KING Framework

Toolkit for Brothers in Leadership

The process of becoming a king in the leadership game is one of constant evolution, growth, mistakes, unlearning, and relearning. *King* offers a four-part leadership framework to help you transform the leader you *are* into the leader *you are destined to be*.

From an abolitionist lens, the KING approach provides a framework for black male leaders to explore the following questions:

1. To what extent do I live a mission-aligned professional life – one that influences real change? How can I lead in a way that always corresponds with my personal North Star?

2. What are some ways I can better leverage my **authentic** leadership? How can I leverage **all** of who I am for equity and justice? How can I speak my truth, no matter who is in the room?

3. In what ways am I maximizing my impact? What are my technical and adaptive superpowers?

4. What self-imposed hurdles stand in the way of me being my very best self?

5. How will I continue prioritizing well-being and joy – both professionally and personally?

In the next four chapters, we will explore each of the four pillars of the KING Leadership Framework.

Each chapter will have the following components:

- **The Main Point.** The *"primary preaching assignment."*
- **The Illustrative Scenario.** A personal story or anecdote connected to the main point of the chapter.
- **KING Moves.** The KING Moves are the actions that we recommend as part of the KING Framework.
- **Reflection Questions.** These questions extend your understanding of the KING Framework and help you personalize it.
- **Quotes for Kings.** Reflect on the quotes and consider how they might apply to your own leadership.

Know who you are.
Know who you can be.
Then, strive to be more than who you are.
Then, be more than you ever thought you could be…

Four-Part Leadership Framework for Black Men

ONE

Know the King Within

The Main Point

Emotional Intelligence (EQ) speaks to perceiving, managing, monitoring, and regulating both emotions and relationships. Researchers on the topic of leadership suggest that Emotional Intelligence has a greater impact on leadership than "traditional" intelligence does. Simply put, in leadership, **EQ > IQ.**

Emotional Intelligence has both external and internal components to it. To effectively lead others, you must first be able to focus on yourself. It's that "you against you" thing. As a leader, you must manage, monitor, and regulate yourself and your own emotions. Please note that I did not say *bury* your emotions. While leading others, you must first prioritize a strong sense of self-awareness, coupled with intentional introspection (also known as mindfulness). You must explore all the ways to possibly know the king within. **Who are you right now, and what does it look like when you are your "supreme self?"**

In the book, *Emotional Intelligence: Why It Can Matter More Than IQ*, Dr. Daniel Goleman underscores the importance of self-awareness. He states very simply that, "...self-awareness is the building block of emotional intelligence." There are several benefits to being self-aware, including the following:

- It can make us more proactive, boost our acceptance, and encourage positive self-development.
- Self-awareness allows us to see things from the perspective of others, practice self-control, work creatively and productively, and experience pride in ourselves and our work, as well as general self-esteem.
- It leads to better decision-making (Ridley, Schutz, Glanz, & Weinstein, 1992).
- It can make us better at our jobs, better communicators in the workplace, and enhance our self-confidence and job-related wellbeing (Sutton, Williams, & Allinson, 2015).

A self-aware leader is cognizant of the good, the bad, and the ugly parts of his leadership. Not only should we be keenly aware of our leadership superpowers, but we should also be clear about our shortcomings and our opportunities for growth. Seek out, embrace, and then act upon the critical feedback. Critical feedback helps us see our true leadership selves. Having a 360–degree view of your personal and professional self has a myriad of positive impacts on your influence as a leader.

In full transparency, I avoided receiving tough, critical feedback for much of my leadership career. There were parts of my leadership profile that I wanted to ignore. If I ignored my flaws, maybe they would go away. Even worse, maybe I wanted to ignore the feedback in an effort to preserve fragile parts of my ego and self-concept.

In the summer of 2014, I was presented with feedback that was extremely painful to my ego and caused me considerable cognitive dissonance. However, this feedback made me more self-aware and a more effective and introspective leader who regularly seeks feedback, especially the most critical feedback.

The Illustrative Scenario

After being an education leader in the St. Louis area for more than two decades, I felt a strong need to recharge my professional battery. I decided to explore leadership opportunities outside of my region. In the summer of 2014, I was hired by the Achievement School District (Memphis) to serve as the founding Director of Strategic Partnerships. At that time, I experienced my first painfully jarring bout of professional trauma. I would imagine that one of Mike Tyson's powerful uppercuts could not hurt any less.

As part of my transition to my role in Memphis, I was required by my employer to participate in a 360-degree feedback process. For the first part of the feedback process, I was charged with posing three broad questions to 20 colleagues and trusted friends:

1. What are Ian's most evident strengths?
   - In what scenario have you seen him demonstrate at least one of the strengths you identified?
2. What are Ian's areas of improvement?

- Do you think he is aware of these improvement areas? Explain.

3. What should Ian start, stop, and/or continue?

In the second part of the 360-degree feedback process, a different set of colleagues and trusted friends were asked to complete an electronic survey. I completed a similar survey as well. In essence, the electronic survey required me and other participants to assess how my leadership shows up in high-stress situations and low-stress situations, respectively.

When the results were finally synthesized and shared with me, I was overwhelmed with a variety of conflicting emotions. I felt a sense of affirmation and pride about the strengths that individuals identified – especially those that I didn't see previously.

In the main, though, I felt deflated, embarrassed, angry, and betrayed. Because I had never seen myself in some of the ways in which I was described, I looked for justifications and ways to explain away the negative feedback. Like many of us who receive anonymous feedback, I tried to attach a person to each piece of unflattering feedback. I continued to say things like, "Who said that shit about me?" or, "Well, I knew they were haters anyway. They just want my spot." I also said things like, "They just don't understand the full story. They don't see things from my point of view."

As I continued to reflect on the comprehensive feedback, I would eventually move to the fifth stage of grief: acceptance. Initially, it was tough to read the feedback I considered to be "negative;" however, once I was able to confront my ego and insecurities, I felt empowered and more self-aware than ever.

When I took a hard look in the mirror and began to deeply reflect on my leadership, I walked away with a few key takeaways:

- As hip-hop artist J Cole says, "Pride is the devil." Pride and ego are counterproductive to leadership. Much of our ego and pride as black men is rooted in what researchers call the *cool pose* – an unconscious response to racism and marginalization. It is a self-protective stance, but it impacts our ability to show up as our full leadership selves. Feedback can chip away at our ego because it exposes some of the flaws we try to hide or ignore…for self-preservation.

- Vulnerability (not fragility) and trust go hand in hand. When leaders demonstrate authentic vulnerability, it empowers others to also be vulnerable. When we are vulnerable, honest, and authentic, it allows our teams to support us in ways they may not have considered before. Equally as important, when we are genuinely vulnerable, our teams give us more grace when we come up short. The challenge is to define what vulnerability looks like for you, given your identities and life experiences.

- Leaders who intentionally create space for mutual, critical feedback will build stronger, more effective teams and more joyful learning environments.

When we see feedback as the "food of champions," we grow.

- Leaders show up very differently and less effectively when we are stressed...and typically don't see how our leadership shifts. When I get stressed, I tend to retreat from my colleagues and work in isolation until my eyes roll in the back of my head. I spend almost every waking hour either *working* or *thinking about working.* I also tend to retreat from personal contact. Instead, I opt for impersonal emails, staff memos, and text messages. Sometimes, I communicate in a tone can come across as dismissive.

- There can be no leadership roses without thorns. It's just part of the process. I can appreciate both the roses and thorns equally now. I clearly see my leadership roses. I am a leader who inspires others, treats people humanely, and demonstrates an unrelenting commitment to excellence and equity; however, I tend to mask my insecurities and flaws with ego, pride, and sometimes humor. I also retreat and become unapproachable when I get overwhelmed.

In summary, the leadership lesson is simple. To lead others, we must first manage, monitor, and regulate ourselves. Emotional Intelligence (EQ)is a fundamental leadership building block, and it starts with self-awareness. As part of the journey towards self-awareness, we must also be open and responsive to the critical feedback that helps us see our full leadership selves.

King Moves

To more deeply explore and leverage the king within, consider the following King Moves:

Actively seek feedback. I must be honest here, my kings. In my experience as a school and school district leader, I have found that many of us are either resistant to or indifferent about feedback. This is not to suggest that there are no sound reasons for not valuing feedback from some folks. I, too, have been resistant to professional feedback at times, as I have found it to be lacking in actionability, inaccurate, and/or overly complimentary. At other times, I have received feedback as overly critical, or simply just without merit because of racial or gender differences. I encourage you to seek out *all* the feedback. Then, eat the meat and leave the bones.

The Proverbs 27:17 scripture has served as both inspiration and aspiration for me as it relates to the value of feedback. It reads, *"As iron sharpens iron, so one man sharpens another."* As a leader, I interpret that scripture to suggest that critical feedback and collegiality sharpen all parties involved. In leadership work, we must seek feedback at every opportunity, no matter the professional circumstance. Experience is indeed a great teacher, and I have become convinced that actively seeking out **all** feedback is essential to each leader's journey. What separates good from great leaders is their ability to **discern** the feedback. In short, great leaders have a "feedback filter." Great leaders inhale all of the feedback, exhale the toxic parts, and move forward on the actionable parts of the feedback.

To make sense of feedback, consider any of the ten questions below:

1. From the feedback, what new lesson did I learn about myself and how I lead?
2. What was affirmed/confirmed for me?
3. How does my body react when I receive painful feedback? What is my body telling me?
4. What does the feedback say about my leadership strengths? What should I do more regularly, consistently, and/or strategically?
5. What are the growth areas I can address right now?
6. Are there some technical/executive skills that I need to develop or enhance?
7. What additional questions do I have?
8. What feedback do I need to further investigate?
9. What should I stop, start, and continue?
10. How can others support my improvement efforts?

Get clear on your personal and professional superpowers. Sometimes, the things we do well naturally are not clear to us.

To get clear on your superpowers:

- Ask friends and colleagues, "When is a time when you have seen me at my best?"
- Take "strengths" assessments like the HIGH5 Strengths test[i] or StrengthsFinders[ii].
- Reflect on all of the academic, professional, and technical training you've had. Brainstorm a list of all the skills and competencies you have in your toolbelt.

Know your EQ. EQ is a combination of self-awareness, self-regulation, motivation, and empathy. To gauge where you stand on the EQ continuum, take an assessment like the Global Leadership Foundation Emotional Intelligence Test[iii].

Be keenly aware of your self-saboteurs. The brain is hardwired with a "fight, flight, or freeze" instinct that is designed to shield us from the possibility of hurt, harm, or danger – either physical or psychological. There are times, however, when the brain misperceives threats. For example, if a person needs a heart or kidney transplant, the body will initially try to reject the organ, even though it will sustain life. The same thing happens when the brain feels a threat to the ego or self-concept – it attempts to protect us. Sometimes, the protection is helpful, but these protective efforts are often unnecessary and limit our ability to be our best. Instead of helping us, the protective efforts hurt us.

Researchers call these self-limited efforts and mindsets self-saboteurs. Positive Intelligence describes saboteurs as, "…the voices in your head that generate negative emotions in the way you handle life's everyday challenges. They represent automated patterns in your mind for how to think, feel, and respond. They cause all of your stress, anxiety, self-doubt, frustration, restlessness, and unhappiness. They sabotage your performance, wellbeing, and relationships."[iv]

Self-sabotaging mindsets, beliefs, and behaviors kick in when you feel a psychological threat. You may learn more about the top nine ways of self-sabotage by taking the Positive Intelligence Saboteur Assessment[v].

Reflection Questions

1. Who am I?
2. Who am I becoming?
3. What are six words or phrases that best describe my strengths? What environments help me best leverage my strengths?
4. What are some of my areas of growth? Do I need to make technical changes (skillset, knowledge)? Should I make adaptive changes (mindset, beliefs, assumptions, motivations)?
5. What are some ways my self-limiting beliefs, mindsets, and behaviors stand in the way or prevent me from reaching my full leadership potential?

Quotes for Kings

"When I discover who I am, I'll be free."
~Ralph Ellison

"We at war with racism. We at war with terrorism. Most of all, we at war with ourselves."
~Kanye West

"Our leadership is just we ourself."
~Queen Claudette Colvin

TWO

Inspire Greatness in Others for Collective Impact

♦ ♦ ♦

The Main Point

The research is crystal clear, and my years of experience prove it to be true: high impact leaders understand the importance of helping others reach their full potential. What becomes crystal clear from the research is that the most impactful leaders inspire greatness in others by doing three primary things well. Written in no particular order, **impactful leaders motivate, model, and coach.**

First, to motivate others towards collective impact, you must understand culture-building is a crucial executive skill. There are "levels" to the science and art of culture-building. It takes a fusion of evidence-based practices, experience, and improvisation to successfully motivate others and build a strong culture. Organizational culture-building is grounded in mutual respect, a shared mission, personal accountability, and trust.

Modeling, the second necessary practice, speaks to the ongoing effort to embody leadership **excellence** – not leadership **perfection**. There are aspects of your leadership that others should **see** in order to **be**; however, while you strive to be an exemplar of excellence, you must remember that leadership is public, not perfect.

As leaders, we know that we will not get everything right. No one does. You will not be on top of your game in every aspect of leadership. We understand that consistent perfection is impossible. To demonstrate the commitment to progress over perfection, we must model vulnerability. We must also embrace critical feedback, be transparent about growth areas, and speak our respective truths.

Operating from a place of honesty and vulnerability creates an organizational culture of authenticity and genuine concern for the greater good. As a result, others around us are inspired to be just as vulnerable. We then can move closer to our collective goals more quickly and less painfully.

Finally, in addition to motivating and modeling, impactful leaders use a warm **and** demanding coaching approach. Like a hard-nosed physical trainer, the best leaders are coaches - not mediocre coaches, but coaches who stretch others beyond their self-imposed limitations. Impactful coaches help others develop the mindsets, beliefs, and practices that sustain positive results.

We must view the practice of coaching as a necessary executive leadership skill. Leaders who are adept at coaching and capacity-building can accelerate impact. Hierarchical, top-down leadership approaches simply do not work. Distributed, democratic leadership approaches allow us to develop powerful teams that suffocate egocentric, self-centric efforts and individuals.

In summary, we are failing in leadership if we are not inspiring others to see themselves as game-changers who matter. By coaching, modeling, and motivating those we serve and lead, we can inspire greatness *fasho*. The excellence and greatness we inspire has one purpose: to create systems where all humans can have access to the life they deserve.

The Illustrative Scenario

Great leaders can inspire others to run through a brick wall. I have discussed three keys to maximizing your leadership impact: a) modeling personal excellence; b) building a culture that motivates others to excellence; and c) providing adaptive coaching support. While I have witnessed several leaders execute these three competencies at a high level, few do it better than Brittany Packnett Cunningham. Sister Brittany is a high-impact, highly committed and humane sister. At a relatively young age, she has shouldered a great deal of accountability and responsibility...along with a heavy dose of hate. Through it all, she models hope and tenacity.

Brittany swims with the sharks and tangles with the tigers for our people, and she is a leadership exemplar in many ways. This is not to say that she is a **perfect** servant, but it is to say that she's a helluva **public** servant. Even President Barack Obama recognized her gangsta. Upon meeting her, he recognized her brilliance, passion, and strategic thinking, comparing her to the late John Lewis. This gives you some insight into the dope sister that BP is.

At one point in my career, I had the privilege and great responsibility to swim in the shark-infested waters alongside her. My leadership will never be the same due to the time I shared with Brittany. When you know greatness, you just know it. *Game recognize game.*

In the summer of 2012, Brittany was hired to take on the role of Executive Director at Teach For America-St. Louis (TFA). As Brittany entered the TFA leadership role, I had just completed my first year as the organization's Director of Strategic Partnerships. As my direct supervisor and junior by more than a decade, Brittany was charged with holding me accountable to my goals by providing feedback, coaching, resources, and general support.

As Brittany was onboarded into the organization, I was looking forward to working alongside my sister. I am sure that being the supervisor of an "old head" was not something Brittany anticipated when she applied for the role. We both may have been a bit uneasy before meeting, but that dissolved the second we formally met. After about ten minutes of conversation, we "understood the assignment" and were fully committed to the mission.

As the months flew by, the professional relationship between the two of us began to grow. There was mutual respect, role clarity, and synergy that inspired me to want to do more, do better, and be better. As time progressed, we sharpened each other as colleagues, but I definitely left Brittany more sharpened than she left me.

Because of our age difference, Brittany affectionately refers to me as Uncle Ian. That demonstration of respect is a direct result of her black church, preacher's kid upbringing. It is that black church, preacher's kid upbringing that imbued her with a moral North Star that guides her leadership journey. It is that black church upbringing that cultivated that special something inside of her that inspires Uncle Ian and countless others.

I was inspired by Brittany because she spoke truth to power in such a way that belied her then-youngish age. I observed her courageously and confidently advocate for our kids and our people. I witnessed her challenge the white racist practices and white racist mindsets – even if it meant losing white racist money and white liberal friends. When working alongside **our** people, I saw her operate with humility, respect, and a moral compass that stayed focused on the prize – even if that meant disagreeing with some of us around issues as diverse as community policing, school choice, faith, sexuality, and politics.

In summary, great leaders inspire greatness in others. As a result of working alongside Brittany Packnett Cunningham, I left with a greater sense of hope, coupled with an unyielding commitment to "the work." Her greatness as a leader inspired me and countless others.

King Moves

As leaders, we all inspire others – both consciously and unconsciously. As leaders, how can we each leverage our individual leadership superpowers so that our work leads to collective impact?

If you want to best inspire greatness in others, consider the following King Moves:

Learn

- Strive to be the lead learner in your organization. Learn as much as you can…and then learn some more. Find both traditional and nontraditional ways to learn and grow.
- Learn about your team's individual and collective strengths. Affirm and acknowledge strengths at every relevant opportunity.
- Learn to take your foot off the gas when you should. Inspire others to do the same.
- Learn about "your people." You should know something meaningful about all the folks that are your direct reports and your managers. At the very least, learn about what matters to them and what inspires them to do the work.

Listen

- Seek feedback from a variety of stakeholders, even if you do not value their opinions.
- Listen to your body. Your body keeps score on life, and it can help you make decisions…if you listen.

Create

- Create spaces for vulnerability by modeling it.
- Create a healthy environment where disagreement and conflict are considered essential for

organizational growth. Create the space for people to "bang it out," then "hug it out."

- Create a system that normalizes smart risk-taking and innovation.
- Create a system that focuses on both collective and individual results...and make the results public.

Build

- Build structures to confront team dysfunction.
- Build structures that decentralize and democratize leadership.
- Build in practices that inspire wellness, joy, and balance.

Reflection Questions

1. How have you inspired others?
2. Who are the people that inspire you, and what are the values or strengths you see in each of them?
3. What do you know about the values of those who work closest to you? How do their values influence how they work?
4. What are your team's individual and collective strengths? Are there specific times when those strengths are most evident?
5. If we secretly recorded you engaging with those whom you manage, would we see more coaching, more directing, or more modeling? Elaborate.

Quotes for Kings

"If your actions inspire others to dream more, learn more, and become more, you are a leader."
~John Quincy

"Black men are ten times greater than they appear against the backdrop of today's world."
~Susan Taylor

"Steel sharpens steel. I'ma keep it real."
~Beanie Siegel

THREE

Navigate North

The Main Point

As leaders, we want our work to be guided by our personal values, beliefs, and morals. We also want to invest our attention, energy, and focus in areas that best align with our North Star, or our **why**. While other things may change around us, our North Star is the constant, ever-present sentiment that inspires, affirms, and grounds us.

For leaders committed to justice, navigating north (the title of this chapter) means that our **why** drives the **what** and the **how**. Our actions should be parallel with our North Star and our personal belief system. When you lose sight of your North Star, your actions, behaviors, and decisions can be out of sync with your personal mission and who you *say* you are. This dissonance tends to result in a continuous state of being unwell. *You'll be all f'd up.*

As a leader, your North Star is a synthesis of your personal mission, vision, values, and goals. When it is time to make a difficult decision, have a difficult conversation, or confront a difficult task, a quick reflection on your North Star can be powerful. It can provide the clarity, courage, and confidence that helps you move forward when it gets tough.

Far too often, though, we work alongside others or in environments that do not share similar values, beliefs, and/or guiding principles. As a result, we feel unnecessary dissonance, regret, and professional trauma. We continue to ignore one simple truism. **It is impossible for leaders of color to thrive in spaces that don't share common values, beliefs, and principles – especially around issues related to equity and race.**

All of your leadership work should align to a North Star, one grounded in a commitment to equity and justice. As a leader, you must seek out and create environments that allow you to be you. If you do not engage in purpose-driven work, you will be eternally miserable and ineffective. Unfortunately, you will waste precious time doing work that does not lead to equity and justice for our people. Instead of changing the *status quo*, your leadership supports it.

I regrettably took on leadership roles that were incompatible with my most important core values, beliefs, and guiding principles. The role that was most in conflict with my North Star was the founding Director of Strategic Partnerships for the Achievement School District. When I was faced with moral challenges, I was confronted with three choices – fight, flee, or freeze. I chose to freeze…then *I fled like a MF*!

I would not wish the professional and personal trauma I experienced on my worst enemy (maybe except Pres 45). At the same time, the valuable lesson I learned was that the universe will get in alignment with you if you make decisions aligned with a righteous North Star.

The Illustrative Scenario

In June of 2014, after being an education leader for more than two decades in the St. Louis region, I took a professional leap of faith. I moved to Memphis to become the founding Director of Strategic Partnerships for the Achievement School District (ASD), a unique school district model, created by the governor of Tennessee. As a leader settling into his 40s, I was excited to accept this position for two primary reasons. First, I thought I would play a significant leadership role in an innovative school district model that could have a **sustainable** positive impact on the lives of thousands of black children. Few traditional school systems that educate predominantly black/brown students have sustained significant academic growth over time. I wanted to be a part of something special.

Not only did I want to take a role that would make a measurable difference for our young people, but the move to Memphis had a spiritual component to it as well. I felt like I was continuing my justice journey in a place where my idol breathed his last (government-complicit) breath. Dr. King advocated for one generation. I would have the opportunity to advocate for the next generation. I got next…or so I thought.

From my second-floor office in downtown Memphis, I could see the Lorraine Motel balcony where Dr. King was murdered. I just knew this was a sign from the Most High. It said that I was moving in a right and righteous direction. It said that I was doing work that directly moved me toward my North Star. This role had my name on it, and Dr. King, the gifted leader whom I most respect and admire, had metaphysically endorsed it. I got next...or so I thought.

Specific aspects of the Achievement School District's vision, distributed leadership model, and caliber of the executive leadership team attracted me to the role, and I deeply believed it would place me on the path toward my life's mission. First, the superintendent (John Doe) set an audacious, almost scary vision. He pledged to exponentially improve student achievement within an unbelievably short period of time. Specifically, in less than five years, he envisioned moving chronically low-performing schools from the bottom fifth percentile of performance to the top ninetieth percentile in performance. *In less than five years...ain't nobody ever done that.*

John Doe's performance guarantee made anyone who understands change management say, "Is this guy nuts? What does he know that we don't know?" He promised a feat unheard of in traditional public school systems across urban America. I thought: **He had accomplished a similar feat in another region of the country, so why couldn't he do it in Memphis? Why not join his squad?**

Also, when the superintendent spoke about his vision, he did it with a passion, confidence, and commitment that resonated with others and made them (and me) want to work alongside him. He spoke about schools as tools of empowerment and agency. He spoke about the importance of school quality, school choice, and parent voice. He provided Memphis education leaders the opportunity to co-design, co-create, and lead their own schools.

Based on the way the superintendent's North Star resonated in my soul, I thought I was getting in the right seat and on the right bus by joining his team. In addition to having a super sharp superintendent at the helm, the district was being co-led by a team of exceptionally sharp, accomplished leaders. I was joining a school district iteration of the 1992 NBA Dream Team, and I was excited about the possibilities for collective impact.

There were some aspects of the district's approach that resonated with me, especially when I was initially onboarded. Then, after the first couple of months, the professional honeymoon would end abruptly. As I began to engage more with the general community and do my due diligence, I uncovered some aspects of my role and the district's approach that conflicted with my moral compass. While the superintendent and his team were awesome human beings, some things just did not feel right. I began to see how our leadership was complicit in supporting the *status quo*. When I first took the role at the ASD, I thought this was the revolutionary next step I was looking for. I would eventually realize that *I wasn't doin' shit* but participating in a system that was broken - no different than the one it sought to replace.

There were two specific aspects of the district's approach and my role that challenged my moral compass. First, I felt that the district's approach to parent engagement was misleading. The ASD presented itself as a quality alternative to Memphis' traditional public schools. From my vantage point, it appeared to me that the district sold the community a dream – by strategically leveraging the social capital of highly regarded parents and community members who had sampled and enjoyed the ASD Cool-Aid.

As part of the district's aggressive growth strategy, the district recruited and trained well-regarded community members to advocate to their families and friends on behalf of the ASD. These well-meaning, loving Memphians were enlisted to advocate for a false choice…and they did a helluva job at it. They were unknowing participants in a shell game. It was the good old bait and switch.

It ripped me apart inside to suspect that I was working for a white-led organization that enlisted well-meaning, mostly poor, mostly black parents to advocate for an unproven school model. I got caught in the Matrix, and it felt terrible.

There is one additional part of the ASD's approach that significantly challenged my moral compass. The district's implicit theory of change was grounded in deficit thinking as it relates to black and brown people living in the hood. Within the deep, dark crevices of the organization, I sensed a white supremacy-inspired belief that black folks *need* white folks (specifically white men) to solve their problems. From my lived experiences, I surmised that the ASD was founded under the premise that black people are inept and that their schools need to be fixed. It was the "black, brown, and broken," pathology perspective that I sensed.

In closing, I was drawn to aspects of the ASD, so I accepted a leadership role within the organization. Because of the superintendent's vision for black and brown students, his passion for his beliefs, and the district's talented executive leadership team, I moved from a comfortable leadership role in my hometown to take on a new challenge in Memphis. After a couple of months on the job, I began to experience deep moral conflict.

Here's my point. When you encounter deep moral conflict, you have to move in conjunction with your North Star. When I deeply reflected on my North Star in relation to my role with the ASD, I had three choices; I could fight, I could fly, or I could flee. I chose to flee. I could not bear the internal conflict. **I left the role after a year.**

King Moves

To stay grounded in your North Star, we recommend the following:

Create an MVVG Compact. MVVG stands for mission, vision, values, and goals.

- **Mission.** Why do I exist? What is my purpose?

Example: My mission is to provide gold standard coaching and consulting supports that help great leaders become their greatest selves.

- **Vision**. If I am successful, beyond even my own wildest dreams, what will be true?

Example: I may not change the world, but I will inspire and influence the ones who will.

- **Values**. What are the 3-5 core values that make up my moral foundation? What 3-5 core values are most important to me – as a human being, not just as a professional?

Example: I value equity, excellence, engagement, strategy, and wellness.

- **Goals**. What will I accomplish?

By June 2022, I will provide executive coaching to 10 leaders, and at least 7 of them will provide evidence that the coaching experience supported their growth.

Write a life's purpose statement that will serve as a written synthesis of your MVVG Compact. Write a one-sentence life purpose statement using the following sentence stem:

I am _____ (descriptor of your "sacred self") who will _____ (describe your desired impact…make it scary and big!)

Example: I am the black king who may not change the world but will touch a million minds, hearts, and hands along the journey.

Create a "moral Mt. Rushmore" that will help you stay focused on your North Star. Create a list of four individuals that bring you back to your **why** when you need to remember it.

Note: If you identify living individuals, you do not need to physically contact these individuals for counsel. Instead, you will "channel" their perspectives at the appropriate times during your leadership journey. The roles are below.

Cheerleader: The perpetual encourager – even when you are wrong.

Challenger: Gives you a healthy push – even when you do not solicit it.

Critic: Offers truthful, brutally honest, and sometimes even harsh feedback. Even if hearing it can be painful, there is always a grain of truth in the criticism.

Conscience: Provides a perspective grounded in what is right and just.

Reflection Questions

1. As a professional, what is most important to you?
2. When were your work responsibilities best aligned with your core values and beliefs?
3. What organizational values are most important to you? Why?
4. What traits do you value most in others? Why?
5. Other than salary, what are some factors that cause leaders to stay in roles that are incompatible with their core values and beliefs?

Quotes For Kings

"Your life purpose is your North Star in the dark night as you navigate your canoe. It is the compass by which your soul directs your life journey."
~Ishak Beery

"Even in the face of disadvantages and dysfunction, you can't let anybody define, control, or take away your vision of your life...not your mother, brother, sister, father, spouse..."
~Mariah Carey

"Y'all think small. I think Biggie."
~Jay Z

FOUR

Gravitate to Great

The Main Point

Over the course of my career, I have worked alongside a number of highly motivated, extremely driven leaders. Motivation and drive, however, can be inspired by a need for popularity, visibility, or acceptance. That type of egocentric leadership should not be confused with purpose-driven, people-driven leadership. Ego-driven leadership, unfortunately, is far too common. Dr. King spoke about this leadership phenomenon more than a half-century ago.

In a speech in February of 1968, at Atlanta's Ebenezer Baptist Church, Dr. King was very deliberate about not vilifying the ego-centric leadership archetype. While he acknowledged the potentially destructive nature of the leadership archetype, he did not fully dismiss the leadership approach. Instead, he called it a natural "drum major instinct" – something inside all of us. If we can harness it, he argued, we can hasten our quest for justice and freedom.

In his speech, Dr. King acknowledged that all of us have a psychological need to feel valued and highly regarded. In the name of justice and the greater good, though, Dr. King offered us a nuanced way of thinking about this drum major instinct. Instead of leveraging the drum major instinct for individual gain and reward, King challenged us to operate as drum majors for justice and freedom. He said, "Yes, if you want to say that I was a drum major, say that I was a drum major for justice. I was a drum major for righteousness, and all of the other shallow things will not matter."[vi]

The point is simple. Game-changing leaders operate from the "leadership as service" perspective, instead of an egocentric perspective. This approach inspires others to model similar transformational leadership behaviors. As a result of modeling this type of leadership stance, the impact of your leadership approach is broadened and deepened.

Game-changing leaders also spend purposeful time in communal spaces with those who have similar missions and passions. In fact, game-changing leaders "cypher" with a diverse spectrum of leaders – all who inspire, affirm, support, challenge, and/or model in a way that builds collective greatness.

Top-tier leaders gain inspiration from others who demonstrate excellence. Oftentimes, the universe will conspire to connect these mission-aligned human beings. Almost instinctively, great leaders begin to nurture authentic, symbiotic professional relationships with others who embody the extraordinary vision, undeniable purpose, or an unyielding commitment to excellence. Yep, **game recognize game.**

In his book, *The 21 Irrefutable Laws of Leadership*, John Maxwell speaks to the **game recognize game** phenomenon. John Maxwell's Law of Magnetism states, "Consciously or not, we tend to attract people who share at least a few of our core characteristics."

I am aware of several transformational leaders who attract other leadership all-stars. Dr. Sharonica Hardin-Bartley is one of those leaders. Her leadership presence has profoundly influenced my leadership journey. She continues to be an exemplar of a high-impact leader who attracts other leadership gangstas.

The Illustrative Scenario

In the late spring of 2016, I began a conversation with superintendent Dr. Sharonica Hardin-Bartley about a potential leadership role on her executive leadership team (cabinet). At the time, I was at the tail end of my participation in the School Systems Leaders Fellowship (SSLF), an 18-month experience that prepares middle-level education leaders for executive leadership roles. Living and working in Memphis at the time, I had just begun aggressively seeking out executive/cabinet-level opportunities, interviewing for roles in cities like Tulsa, Las Vegas, DC, Denver, and Boston. I was nervous about making another professional transition, but I was also extremely excited.

As the interviews and potential offers started coming from different school districts, I was holding out for the right opportunity. In my mind, this was the ideal time to make a professional power move! The opportunity to work in DC with then-superintendent Dr. Kaya Henderson was a most attractive possibility at one point, but the opportunity to return to the STL to work alongside my long-time friend, Dr. Sharonica Hardin-Bartley, was extremely exciting. Sharonica had demonstrated her greatness over the course of her career, and other exceptional leaders have proven to be attracted to that greatness. Some of the top leaders around the region were vying to be on her newly forming "dream team."

I dedicated an inordinate number of hours preparing myself to jump through the hoops of the interview process. I was not certain I would be hired for the role, but I would eventually be hired as the Assistant Superintendent (Chief Academic Officer) in The School District of University City. Throughout the interview process, I was clear about one thing: I wanted to support Sharonica's vision and leadership. As the interviewing and hiring process evolved, I realized that so many people felt the same way I did.

Over the course of a few years, Sharonica assembled a team of all-stars who attracted other all-stars. One of the most impressive aspects of Hardin-Bartley's leadership presence is that others are inspired to work alongside her. She operates from a human-centered, student-first perspective. Ego is nowhere in her leadership equation. As a systems leader, she provides a fair balance of support and accountability. Great leaders can thrive in an environment like the one Dr. Hardin-Bartley creates. Game recognize game, and a variety of all-stars want to be on Hardin-Bartley's team.

There is a leadership lesson to be learned from Hardin-Bartley's approach. When we serve selflessly, embody excellence, and insist on greatness, other leaders see that. Operating with a service orientation is a sign of true leadership, and other true leaders recognize that as well. When servant leaders see other service leaders, they are inspired and motivated to work alongside them. Who doesn't want to play with Lebron, Kobe, or MJ?

King Moves

To lead, participate in, and create communities where greatness inspires greatness, we suggest the following King Moves:

First, define greatness. As leaders, we must define great leadership for ourselves. Use the steps below to better define what greatness looks like for you.

- Write the names of five individuals (living or dead) who embody greatness – in any shape, form, or fashion.
- Write down the reasons you consider each of those individuals great. What strengths and/or values do they embody that resonate with you?
- After you have brainstormed a list of strengths and values, highlight the five descriptors that mean the most to you.

- Add to the list, if necessary.
- This is a draft of your definition of greatness.

Next, create a list of the "organizational Mt. Rushmore." Once you have clarity around your vision of great leadership, generate a list of the top four organizations that demonstrate leadership traits that are important to you.

Last, thoughtfully and authentically cultivate professional relationships. As leaders, we attract the energy we put out. Spend purposeful time in community with those who inspire, affirm, support, challenge, and model. Prioritize nurturing symbiotic relationships with those who embody the extraordinary vision, undeniable purpose, or an unyielding commitment to excellence.

Reflection Questions

1. Who are the 3-5 individuals who have inspired you?
2. What did you learn from them that supports your leadership journey?
3. Why do people enjoy working alongside you? How do you intentionally support, inspire, and stretch them?

Quotes for Kings

"Surround yourself by people smarter than you."
~Barack Obama

"One is too small a number to achieve greatness."
~John Maxwell

"Greatness is upon you. You better act like it."
~Dr. Eric Thomas

Conclusion

Life ♦ Legacy ♦ Impact

The KING Leadership Framework is not designed to be prescriptive and formulaic. Instead, it is an adaptive approach designed to push you to think more deeply about your leadership and your life. As you walk away from this book, *King*, you should be able to better respond to the questions below:

- Who am I, and who am I becoming?
- Who do the people I work alongside **think** I am?
- Who do I pretend to be?
- To what extent do I live a mission-aligned life…one that influences and inspires real change?
- When my professional work is in direct alignment with my personal mission and my North Star, what does that look, feel, and sound like?
- What are some of the self-limiting beliefs, mindsets, and behaviors that prevent me from reaching my full leadership potential? In other words, how do I self-sabotage?
- What strengths, gifts, competencies, and/or talents show up most often in my leadership walk? Which ones would I like to show up more?
- What values are most important to me in my workplace?

- What professional environments allow me to be my most authentic and most effective leadership self? What professional environments stifle my leadership?
- What is it about my leadership approach that inspires others to be great?

Live the life you want to live. Leave the legacy you want to leave. Be the king you are destined to be.

References

i www.high5test.com
ii www.gallup.com/cliftonstrengths
iii http://globalleadershipfoundation.com/geit/eitest.html
iv https://www.positiveintelligence.com/saboteurs/
v https://assessment.positiveintelligence.com/saboteur/overview
vi https://www.beaconbroadside.com/broadside/2018/02/martin-luther-king-jrs-the-drum-major-instinct-sermon-turns-50.html

Made in the USA
Monee, IL
18 February 2023

28143419R00051